# STEAM COLOUR PORTFOLIO
## Volume Two

## MIDLAND & EASTERN LINES

## Keith R. Pirt

BOOK LAW PUBLICATIONS

*First published in the United Kingdom by Book Law Publications 2004*
*382 Carlton Hill, Nottingham, NG4 1JA.*
*Printed and bound by The Amadeus Press, Cleckheaton, West Yorkshire.*

# INTRODUCTION

Welcome to the second album in this series, which covers the London Midland and also Eastern Region types, including Scottish scenes as well. All the scenes were captured on film in the late 1950's and early 1960's, using Kodachrome film and high quality 35mm cameras as detailed in Volume I.

Although I did photograph many London Midland locomotive and train scenes, I make no excuses for the fact that I found Eastern (former LNER) types more attractive for photography. Besides, they were nearer to my then home and East Coast Main Line Pacifics were far more abundant. All too soon the ECML expresses were fully timetabled to be dieselised by June 1963 so, a switch was made to photographing London Midland types over the hills! Again all 'working for living' engines - no preserved pets or laid on exhausts.

*Keith R Pirt*
*Chesterfield - June 2004.*

*(opposite)* New England 2-10-0 No.92149 heads an Up fitted cement train past the signals south of Retford crossing in November 1961.

With little more than six months to go before its withdrawal, Royal Scot No.46108 SEAFORTH HIGHLANDER, of Upperby shed, climbs past Skerton with a heavy Down express in July 1962.

With the long cold winter of 1962/63 still enveloping the country, Fowler 4F No.44580 heads towards Birmingham and Worcester at Fladbury with a Down van train in March 1963.

Former Midland IF 0-6-0T No.41734 shunts iron ore tippler wagons in Staveley Iron Works yard under a leaden sky in June 1965.

Mold Junction based Stanier Class 5 No.44986, fitted with a self weighing tender, heads south past Skerton with an Up van train in August 1962.

On a regular duty, Holbeck Royal Scot No.46113 CAMERONIAN pulls away from Dumfries with the Down *THAMES CLYDE EXPRESS* in June 1959. In the station are an exLMS 2P 4-4-0 No.40614, and the preserved Great North of Scotland 4-4-0 No.49.

LMS Ivatt Cl.2 2-6-0 No.46485 pauses at Heeley station Sheffield with the 9.39 a.m. 'all stations' from Sheffield (Midland) to Chinley in October 1965.

Jubilee No.45602 BRITISH HONDURAS heads north past Leyland, south of Preston, with a Down express in June 1964.

Even in unlined black paint, ex MR Class 2P 4-4-0 No.40557 makes a nice portrait as it rests outside Millhouses shed in October 1957.

Duchess No.46240 CITY OF COVENTRY climbs past Skerton with the Down *LAKES EXPRESS* in July 1963. Except for the first month of its life (based at Crewe North for running in), this Pacific spent all of its working life operating from London depots, Camden up to September 1963 and then Willesden for the last year up to withdrawal. On this day 46240 would have worked through from Euston on what was, up to then, a regular Pacific turn.

BR Standard Cl.9F No.92122, passes Sheet Stores junction, Trent with an Up coke train in June 1965.

Longsight, Manchester based Britannia No.70031 BYRON gets away from Hartford station with a Down stopping express in June 1959.

BR Standard Cl.4 No.80127 has just taken on water at Glasgow (Central) station in July 1959 as a Fairburn Cl.4 2-6-4T heads south with a suburban train.

Ex Caledonian Railway 'Jumbo' Cl.2F 0-6-0 No.57246 waits to leave Killin station with the branch train to Killin Junction in July 1959.

Holbeck based Caprotti Cl.5 No.44757 climbs past Dore and Totley with a Newcastle to Bristol express in May 1957.

Rebuilt Patriot 7P No.45512 BUNSEN heads an Up parcels train near Leyland in July 1963.

Stanier Cl.5 No.45169, with St Rollox style numbers, awaits the next call to duty at Dumfries shed in June 1959.

Unnamed Patriot 6P No.45517, of Liverpool Bank Hall shed, has just arrived at York North shed for servicing after working a Liverpool to Newcastle express into the city in May 1959.

Stanier 2-6-0 No.42960, recently ex works, heads an Up excursion near Skerton in August 1962.

Ex MR Johnson half cab Class 1F 0-6-0T No.41804 stands in front of the blast furnaces at Staveley Iron Works, awaiting the next call of duty in June 1965.

BR 9F No.92233 crosses Arten Gill viaduct amidst yellow gorse in bloom with an Up Long Meg to Widnes (ICI) anhydrite train on a glorious day in May 1967.

Britannia No.70024 VULCAN pulls away from Settle station with an Up Carlisle-Leeds parcels train in May 1967.

Class 5 No.44670, of Kingmoor shed, leaves Armathwaite station with the late afternoon Carlisle to Leeds 'all stations' in May 1964.

Ex Caley 2P No.55198 is carriage pilot in the sidings at Inverness in July 1959.

Kentish Town Jubilee No.45616 MALTA G.C. nears Beauchief station on the climb out of Sheffield with an express for St. Pancras in May 1959.

Ex CR Pickersgill 3F 0-6-0 No.57667 nears Kentallen station with the daily Ballachulish to Oban branch freight in July 1959.

Aberdeen Ferryhill based Class 5 No.44703 nears Drumlithie with the 06.40 a.m. Aberdeen to Glasgow semi-fast on a clear July morning in 1966.

Crewe North Royal Scot No.46148 THE MANCHESTER REGIMENT nears Skerton with a Down express in August 1962.

Millhouses based Jubilee No.45725 REPULSE rounds the curve past Dore and Totley as it climbs out of Sheffield with a Sheffield (Midland) to St. Pancras express in May 1957.

BR built Duchess No.46257 CITY OF SALFORD passes Blackford with an Up fish train for London from Aberdeen in June 1964.

Stanier Cl.5 No.45254 darkens the sky crossing Ais Gill viaduct with a Carlisle to Leeds freight in July 1965.

Ivatt Cl.2 2-6-2T No.41245 shunts coal wagons onto the double sided coal stage at Millhouses shed, Sheffield in December 1959.

Princess Royal class 8P Pacific No.46200 THE PRINCESS ROYAL, in clean BR maroon livery, graces the shed yard at Llandudno Junction in May 1962.

Ex MR 4F No.43888 puts up a fine smoke exhaust passing Millhouses engine shed, Sheffield with a Sunday ramblers special, composed of ex LMS stock, bound for Edale in August 1959.

Eastfield based Class 5 No.44787 rolls into Garelochead station with an afternoon train from Fort William to Glasgow (Queen Street) in July 1959. The fireman is ready with the tablet for exchange.

Near Skerton, in July 1962, 'Crab' No.42894 heads a Down meat empties from Broad Street, London to Carlisle.

Stanier Cl.5 No.45044 and an unidentified Jubilee double head an Up Manchester bound express at Euxton Junction in May 1961.

Fowler Cl.4 2-6-4T No.42365 brings a Down Manchester (Central) to Chester (Northgate) 'stopping' train into Northwich in August 1959.

Duchess No.46245 CITY OF LONDON heads the Up *ROYAL SCOT* at Hartford in June 1959.

Two Stanier Class 5's with No.44702 leading, double head the morning express from Fort William to Glasgow (Queen Street) past Arrochar yard in July 1959.

Jubilee No.45593 KOLHAPUR races north past Garsdale with the 'summer only' Nottingham to Glasgow express in July 1967.

BR Cl.5 No.73151, fitted with Caprotti valve gear, runs by the Alan water near Dunblane with a late afternoon express from Glasgow to Dundee in September 1965.

Kirkby-in-Ashfield 8F No.48098 has charge of an Up hopper train at Sheet Stores junction in June 1965.

Class 5 4-6-0 44780 heads home to Llandudno with a Down working between Abergele and Colwyn Bay in June 1963.

Kingmoor 9F No.92015 roars past Ais Gill summit with a Long Meg to Widnes anhydrite train in July 1966.

BR Standard Class 6P 4-6-2 No.72007 CLAN MACKINTOSH is working south of Preston with a Liverpool bound special in August 1964. By this time something of a rarity so far south, this class could regularly be found working Glasgow expresses to both Liverpool and Manchester before the advent of main line diesels.

Gresley A3 No.60110 ROBERT THE DEVIL, fitted with a double chimney and German type smoke deflectors, heads the Up *YORKSHIRE PULLMAN* past Ordsall in February 1962. A rare event as this working was normally a Copley Hill Peppercorn A1 duty.

Class O4/8 2-8-0 No.63728 climbs past Heath siding on the former Great Central main line south of Sheffield, with Up coal empties consisting of 16-ton 'windcutter' wagons in April 1963.

After a general repair, Gresley A4 No.60015 QUICKSILVER, in days old ex works condition, stands in the shed yard at Grantham in May 1959 ready to work home to King's Cross.

Peppercorn A2 No.60530 SAYAJIRAO heads south through the rock cutting at Hilton Junction, Perth with a morning Dundee to Glasgow express in September 1965.

Barely eighteen months old, and having cost £32,845 to build, Swindon built BR Standard 9F No.92201 of Doncaster shed, emerges from Peasecliffe tunnel north of Grantham with a heavy Up ECML freight in June 1960.

Passing through Saltersford cutting, south of Grantham, Thompson A2/3 No.60523 SUN CASTLE of Doncaster shed, heads a King's Cross bound express in August 1962. Exactly one year later this engine was cut up at Doncaster works.

King's Cross A4 No.60026 MILES BEEVOR emerges from Stoke tunnel south of Grantham with a King's Cross to Newcastle express in May 1960.

Two former North Eastern 0-6-0s of LNER Class J27, Nos.65844 and 65846, flank BR 2-10-0 No.92005 inside York shed roundhouse in April 1965. This shed is now part of the National Railway Museum.

Gresley Class K2 No.61794 LOCH OICH is turned on the turntable at Fort William shed in July 1959. Outside the shed stands Thompson Class K1/1 61997 MACCAILIN MOR, which had been rebuilt from a Gresley K4.

A4 No.60027 MERLIN heads an afternoon 3-hour Aberdeen to Glasgow express past Muirton yard, north of Perth, in September 1964.

Ex Great Central 0-6-0, LNER Class J11 No.64397 departs from Grantham with a Nottingham bound 'local' passenger train in June 1959.

After working up to Hull with empties the previous day, King's Cross based Thompson B1 No.61394 heads home with a Hull to King's Cross fish train on a glorious June day in 1960 leaving Peasecliffe tunnel behind.

Gateshead A3 No.60075 ST. FRUSQUIN heads a Down Newcastle express away from York past Leeman Road in October 1959.

York based Peppercorn A1 No.60140 BALMORAL climbs round the curve at Gamston with an Up express to King's Cross in May 1960.

Gresley K3 No.61803, recently ex works after a general repair at Doncaster, heads an eastbound freight at Ordsall on the former GCR line at Retford in May 1959. The locomotive retains the Great Northern type round shank buffers fitted on building in 1920.

Gresley Class V3 2-6-2T No.67619 waits to leave Helensburgh (Central) station with a suburban train to Glasgow (Queen Street Low Level) in July 1959.

LNER built B16/3 4-6-0 No.61463 leaves York with an Up express for Leeds ex Scarborough in August 1959.

Thompson A2/1 No.60501 COCK O' THE NORTH leaves York with a Down Liverpool to Newcastle express at Leeman Road sidings in May 1959.

Ex Great Eastern 2-4-0 (LNER Class E4) No.62785 leaves Fordham Junction with a Mildenhall to Cambridge branch train in May 1958. This was the last 2-4-0 locomotive type at work on British Railways at that time.

Ex Great Northern Class O2 No.63940, complete with GN style cab and tender and recently ex Doncaster works after its last general repair, waits for the next turn of duty at Grantham shed on the last day of August 1962.

Ex North British Railway 0-6-0 No.64577 (LNER Class J37) waits at Wormit station with the Dundee to Tayport branch goods train in June 1965. The River Tay and its famous bridge form a scenic background.

Peppercorn K1 No.62012 is turned on the turntable at Fort William shed prior to working the 4 p.m. train to Mallaig in July 1959. No.62012 arrived on the West Highland line in 1952 but with the introduction of diesel motive power in 1962 it transferred to Alnmouth shed in the North Eastern Region.

Gresley V2 No.60862, rebuilt in 1957 with three separate cylinders, and fitted with a Kylchap double chimney in 1961, passes Retford with the Up 'Scotch Goods' in a snowy and extremely cold landscape in January 1963.

D11 4-4-0 No.62667 SOMME departs from Sheffield in August 1958 with a Cleethorpes bound express and is near Woodburn Road sidings. During 1957 and 1958, all the D11's migrated to Darnall shed with most of them ending their days there after many months in store. During its lifetime, 62667 had been allocated to eighteen sheds with Darnall as the last one. It was condemned on 12th August 1960 and cut up at Doncaster.

Gresley B17 No.61620 CLUMBER nears Woodhouse with the Liverpool to Harwich boat train in August 1958. Shortly after this time the Britannia's took over from the 4-6-0's and the latter were quickly condemned and consigned for scrap. No.61620 was cut up on 25th January 1960.

Ex NBR Class J88 68349 is shed pilot at Eastfield shed, Glasgow in June 1959. All thirty-five engines of this useful class made it into BR ownership with many lasting into the early 1960's, 68349 being one of them but its last year of life was spent at Grangemouth shed and it was cut up at St Rollox works in October 1960.

A3's 60049 GALTEE MORE and 60059 TRACERY stand in the afternoon sun whilst being prepared for main line duties at Grantham shed in May 1959. Shortly after this view was taken, King's Cross based 60059 went into works for its penultimate general overhaul, whilst Grantham shedded 60049 had just received a 'general'. Both Doncaster built engines were condemned in December 1962 and, appropriately, cut up at the 'Plant'.

Haymarket based Peppercorn A2 No.60536 TRIMBUSH, ex works 29th April (its last repair) and running-in from Doncaster, departs from Grantham with a Sunday afternoon 'parley' train to Doncaster in May 1961.

Gresley Class V3 2-6-2Ts 67604 and 67632 grace the shed yard at Helensburgh to the west of Glasgow in June 1959. Both engines were allocated to Parkhead shed in Glasgow and within a few short years would become redundant with the electrification of the Clyde suburban services.

King's Cross A3 No.60109 HERMIT, fitted with double chimney, departs for the south from York with a morning express from Newcastle to London in May 1959. V2 No.60974 is in the background.

Thompson B1 No.61044 departs from Sheffield (Victoria) with a Great Central line express for Nottingham in October 1958.

Darnall J39 No.64890 departs in grand style from Sheffield (Victoria) with a morning excursion to Cleethorpes in July 1959.

In July 1966 J37 No.64547 rests in the yard by Montrose engine shed - a classic sub shed with an old grounded coach body bothie, turntable and coal wagon. The Dundee based J37, suitably decorated like all the other 62B engines at the time, was coming to the end of its working life, being withdrawn on the following New Year's Eve.

Peppercorn A1 No.60156 GREAT CENTRAL climbs Gamston bank, south of Retford, with a Leeds (Central) to King's Cross express in July 1961.

Recently ex works Gresley K2 No.61738, of Colwick shed, departs from Sheffield (Victoria) passing Woodburn sidings with a morning 'all stations' to Nottingham (Victoria) in October 1958.

V2 No.60964 THE DURHAM LIGHT INFANTRY heads south past Hatfield with an express for King's Cross in May 1961.

B16 No.61477, one of the B16's renumbered to make way for the Thompson B1 onslaught, passes under York Holgate bridge, taking the station avoiding line, with a Down freight in May 1959. By the beginning of 1960 this engine would be condemned by and cut up at Darlington works.

C15 No.67474 takes water at Garelochead station with a Craigendoran to Arrochar push-pull train in July 1959.

A4 No.60021 WILD SWAN climbs Gamston bank with an Up express for King's Cross in May 1960.

One of the Great Central built A5's, No.69808 of Boston shed, is ex works on Darlington shed on the 2nd October 1956, after its last repair before withdrawal.

Ex Great Eastern 0-6-0s, Nos.65420 and 65474 of Class J15, await their calls to duty in the yard at March shed in March 1959.

J6 No.64213 departs from Grantham during the late afternoon, with a stopping train for Nottingham (Victoria) in May 1959.

Peppercorn A1 No.60148 ABOYEUR leaves Stoke tunnel with the Up *YORKSHIRE PULLMAN* in August 1962.

Peppercorn A2 No.60532 BLUE PETER heads the Tuesdays and Thursdays Only Up fitted freight from Craiginches (Aberdeen) to Millerhill (Edinburgh) away from the yard at Dundee Tay Bridge in September 1965.

Gresley V2 No.60813, with a stovepipe chimney and small deflectors, nears Broughty Ferry with a 'Saturdays Only' Manchester to Aberdeen express in July 1966. Two months later the V2 was condemned, just a year short of its thirtieth birthday.

Class A1 No.60160 AULD REEKIE pulls away from Retford station with a Down express from King's Cross to Leeds in February 1962. The Pacific was ex works on 30th December 1961 and was undergoing a prolonged running-in period at Doncaster shed before returning north to Auld Reekie (Edinburgh) Haymarket shed. That Doncaster general overhaul was its last repair.

D16/3 No.62589 is the station pilot at March, Cambridgeshire in March 1959. Less than two months from withdrawal, this was about as strenuous a duty as the near fifty year old engine undertook in its final months.

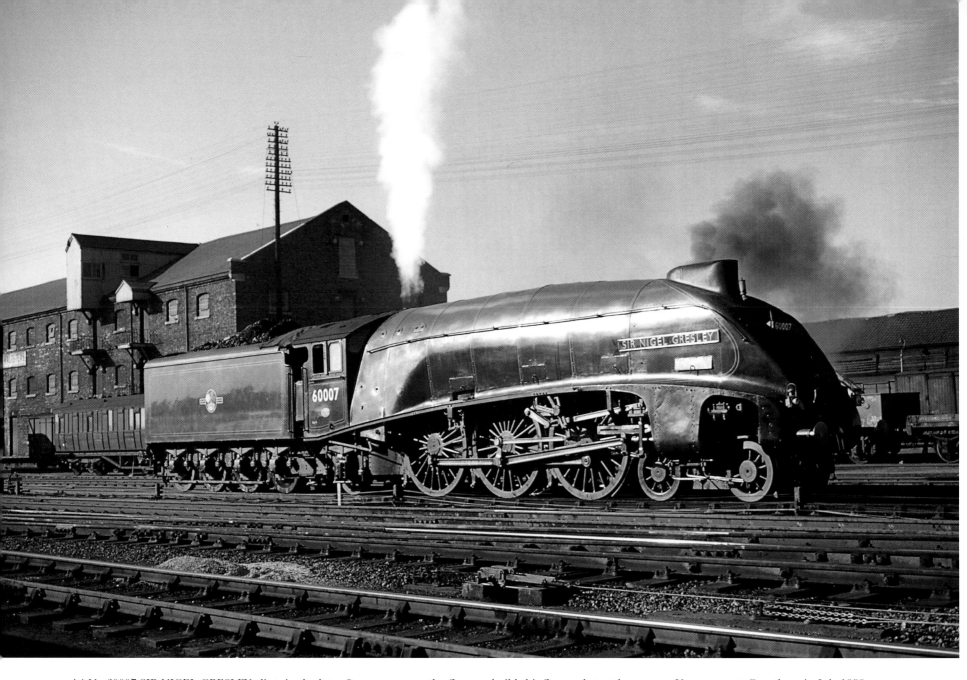

A4 No.60007 SIR NIGEL GRESLEY glints in the late afternoon sun as the fireman builds his fire ready to take over an Up express at Grantham in July 1959.